Henry Purcell

The Music in Dryden's King Arthur

Henry Purcell

The Music in Dryden's King Arthur

ISBN/EAN: 9783337433871

Printed in Europe, USA, Canada, Australia, Japan

Cover: Foto ©Thomas Meinert / pixelio.de

More available books at **www.hansebooks.com**

The Music in
DRYDEN'S
KING ARTHUR

Composed by
HENRY PURCELL

Edited by

J. A. FULLER MAITLAND
for the
BIRMINGHAM FESTIVAL 1897

Price 10/- net
(1951)

III.

INDEX.

Overture .... Page 3

ACT I.
SACRIFICE SCENE.

- N° 1. Solo and Chorus. "Woden, first to thee" ...... " 5
- " 2. Recit. and Chorus. "The lot is cast" ...... " 11
- " 3. Alto Solo and Chorus. "I call, I call you all" ...... " 16

BATTLE SCENE.

- " 4. Tenor Solo and Chorus. "Come if you dare" ...... " 20

ACT II.
SPIRIT SCENE.

- " 5. Symphony ...... " 28
- " 6. Symphony ...... " 28
- " 7. Soprano Solo and Chorus. "Hither this way" ...... " 29
- " 8. Bass Solo. "Let not a moonborn elf" ...... " 34
- " 9. Chorus. "Hither this way" ...... " 36
- " 10. Quintet and Chorus. "Come, follow me" ...... " 38

PASTORAL SCENE.

- " 11. Tenor Solo and Chorus. "How blest are shepherds" ...... " 46
- " 12. Duet. "Shepherd, Shepherd, May invites you" ...... " 51
- " 13. Chorus. "Come shepherds, lead up" ...... " 54
- " 14. Hornpipe ...... " 55

ACT III.
FROST SCENE.

- " 15. Recit. and Solos. *Tenor and Bass.* "What ho! thou genius of the clime" ...... " 56
- " 16. Recitative. "No part of my Dominion" ...... " 62
- " 17. Duet. "Sound a parley, ye fair" ...... " 72
- " 18. Hornpipe ...... " 77

ACT IV.
SYLVAN SCENE.

- " 19. Overture ...... " 78
- " 20. Duet. *2 Sopranos.* "Two daughters of this aged stream" ...... " 80
- " 21. Passacaglia, *with Solos and Chorus.* "How happy the lover" ...... " 83

ACT V.
THE VISION OF BRITAIN.

- " 22. Trumpet Tune ...... " 94
- " 23. Air. "Ye blust'ring brethren of the skies" ...... " 94
- " 24. Symphony ...... " 97
- " 25. Symphony ...... " 99
- " 26. Duet and Chorus. "Round thy coasts" ...... " 100
- " 27. Trio. "For folded flocks" ...... " 103
- " 28. Song. "Your hay it is mow'd" ...... " 106
- " 29. Song. "Fairest Isle, all Isles" ...... " 109
- " 30. Dialogue. "You say 'tis love" ...... " 111

SCENE. THE ORDER OF THE GARTER.

- " 31. Trumpet Tune ...... " 118
- " 32. Song. "Saint George, the Patron of our isle" ...... " 118
- " 33. Chorus. "Our natives not alone appear" ...... " 122
- " 34. The Grand Dance. (Chaconne.) ...... " 124

"KING ARTHUR."

Preface.

The success of Purcell's music to *Dioclesian* and to *Amphitryon* led to his being chosen by Dryden to supply the music for *King Arthur* which was brought out with great success in 1691. Although called at the time "a Dramatick Opera", the music has so little to do with the main action of the piece, that the title is something of a misnomer. The summary of the play incorporated with the words of the vocal portions will show how entirely the musical numbers are subsidiary to the plot.

Like the majority of Purcell's works, the music was not published in his lifetime, and even in the publications issued by his widow within the few years after the composer's death, only a certain proportion of the vocal numbers are to be found. The overture and entr'actes — act-tunes, as they were called — appeared in the Ayres for the Theatre, published in 1697. But a great deal of the music is only to be found in MS. scores, most of them of a comparatively late date, and of varying degrees of correctness. This edition, which I have prepared for the Birmingham Festival of 1897, is based upon a minute critical examination of all the existing MSS. and printed copies that are now to be found. Professor Edward Taylor edited a full score for the Musical Antiquarian Society in 1843 for which he used certain of the MS. authorities mentioned below; his edition did not include the song "Your hay it is mow'd", now printed in this form for the first time. It appears as a single song on a ballad-sheet in the British Museum, in a slightly different version (without Purcell's name), in a famous compilation of Tom d'Urfey's, and in the MS. score of the work in the library of Buckingham Palace, where although the chorus parts are not filled in, their presence is indicated by the arrangement of the written pages. These chorus parts I have ventured to supply conjecturally. Permission to examine the MS. was graciously given by her majesty the Queen. One number occurs in none of the older MSS. authorities that I have seen, viz. the song of Honour in act V. which I have inserted on the authority of Professor Taylor's edition, since from internal evidence it appears to be unquestionably by Purcell. The main authorities are 15 in number, reckoning the collection called "Orpheus Britannicus" and "Ayres for the Theatre" each as one. The thirteen MSS. may be classified as follows:

The earliest MS. score, a fragment containing the first act alone, together with another of the best authorities, is in the library of St. Michael's College, Tenbury; three eighteenth century scores are in the British Museum, an incomplete score is in the library of Christ Church Oxford, a MS. score in Croft's handwriting, in the Fitzwilliam Museum, Cambridge, another of later date is in the Royal College of Music, and the Buckingham Palace score has been already mentioned. For the loan of a score and parts belonging to Gresham College, I am indebted to the present Gresham Professor, Dr. J. F. Bridge, and my thanks are also due to Mr. W. H. Cummings, F. S. A. for the loan of his three MSS. scores.

KING ARTHUR.

The main action of Dryden's play deals with the conquest by King Arthur, "the British Worthy", as he is called in the title, of Oswald, king of Kent, upon St. George's day. The love interest is provided by Emmeline, the blind daughter of the duke of Cornwall, whose sight is restored by Merlin's magic power. The musical numbers are almost entirely incidental, that is, they seldom have anything to say to the main action of the play.

ACT I.

In the first scene Arthur and Emmeline appear, and the former goes off to fight the Saxons with Oswald at their head. The second scene represents a place of heathen worship, before the altars of Woden, Thor, and Freya. Oswald, by the advice of his magician, Osmond, and the latter's "trusty fiend", Grimbald, an "earthy spirit", prepares to sacrifice six Saxons.

SACRIFICE SCENE.

FIRST PRIEST.

Woden, first to thee,
A milk-white steed, in battle won,
We have sacrificed.

CHORUS.

We have sacrificed.

SECOND PRIEST.

Let our next oblation be
To Thor, thy thundering son,
Of such another.

CHORUS.

We have sacrificed.

THIRD PRIEST.

A third (of Friesland breed was he)
To Woden's wife, and to Thor's mother;
And now we have atoned all three.

CHORUS.

We have sacrificed.

TWO PRIESTS.

The white horse neigh'd aloud.
To Woden thanks we render,
To Woden we have vow'd.

CHORUS.

To Woden our defender.

THE ORACLE.

The lot is cast, and Tanfan pleas'd;
Of mortal cares you shall be eas'd.

CHORUS.

Brave souls, to be renown'd in story.
Honour prizing,
Death despising,
Fame acquiring
By expiring;
Die and reap the fruit of glory.

SOLO.

I call you all
To Woden's hall;
Your temples round
With ivy bound,
In goblets crown'd,
And plenteous bowls of burnish'd gold;

Where you shall laugh
And dance and quaff
The juice that makes the Britons bold.

(The Saxons are led off to be sacrificed, but notwithstanding the atonement made to their deities, they are defeated in the battle, which is supposed to be fought behind the scenes "with drums, trumpets, and military shouts and excursions; after which, the Britons, expressing their joy for the victory, sing this song of triumph.")

BATTLE SCENE.

SOLO AND CHORUS.

"Come if you dare", our trumpets sound;
"Come if you dare", the foes rebound;
"We come, we come, we come, we come,"
Says the double, double, double beat of
 the thundering drum.

Now they charge on amain,
 Now they rally again;
The gods from above the mad labour behold,
And pity mankind that will perish for gold.

The fainting Saxons quit their ground.
Their trumpets languish in the sound;
They fly, they fly, they fly, they fly,
"Victoria, Victoria", the bold Britons cry.

Now the victory's won,
 To the plunder we run;
We return to our lasses like fortunate traders,
Triumphant with spoils of the vanquish'd
 invaders.

ACT II.

Philidel, an "airy spirit", formerly one of Osmond's familiars, has refused to decoy the Britons into a morass, and fearing the vengeance of Grimbald for this disobedience, he invokes the powerful magician, Merlin, who descending in a chariot drawn by dragons, charges Philidel to stand beside the "trembling bogs, that bear a greensward show", in order to warn the Britons away to firmer ground. The musical part of the scene represents the contradictory directions given by the spirits attached to Philidel and Gimbald respectively.

SPIRIT SCENE.

PHILIDEL.

Hither this way, this way bend,
Trust not that malicious fiend;

Those are false deluding lights,
Wafted far and near by sprites.
Trust them not, for they'll deceive ye,
And in bogs and marshes leave ye.

CHORUS.

Hither this way, this way bend.

PHILIDEL.

If you step, no danger thinking,
Down you fall, a furlong sinking.
'Tis a fiend who has annoyed ye,
Name but heaven, and he'll avoid ye.

CHORUS.

Hither this way, this way bend.

PHILIDEL'S SPIRITS.

Trust not that malicious fiend.

GRIMBALD'S SPIRITS.

Trust me, I am no malicious fiend. *

GRIMBALD.

Let not a moon-born elf mislead ye
 From your prey, and from your glory;
Too far, alas, he has betrayed ye;
 Follow the flames that wave before ye.
Sometimes seven, and sometimes one;
Hurry, hurry, hurry, hurry on.

See, see the footsteps plain appearing,
 That way Oswald chose for flying,
Firm is the ground, and fit for bearing,
 Where yonder pearly dews are lying.
Far he cannot hence be gone;
Hurry, hurry, hurry, hurry on.

CHORUS.

Hither this way, this way bend.

(The Britons follow Philidel, and Grimbald "sinks with a flash".)

PHILIDEL AND SPIRITS
(Quintet & Chorus).

Come follow, follow, follow me.
And me, and me, and me.
And greensward all your way shall be.
No goblin or elf shall dare to offend ye.

* This line is not set to music.

We brethren of air
You heroes will bear
To the kind and the fair that attend ye.

In the next scene, Emmeline, left alone with her confidante, is entertained with a pastoral song and dance.

PASTORAL SCENE.

Enter Shepherds and Shepherdesses.

SHEPHERD
(Tenor solo & Chorus).

How blest are shepherds, how happy their lasses,
While drums and trumpets are sounding alarms!
Over our lowly sheds all the storm passes;
And when we die, 'tis in each other's arms.
All the day on our herds and flocks employing;
All the night on our flutes and in enjoying.

Bright nymphs of Britain, with graces attended,
Let not your days without pleasure expire;
Honour's but empty, and when youth is ended,
All men will praise you, but none will desire.
Let not youth fly away without contenting;
Age will come time enough for your repenting.

(Here the men offer their flutes to the women, which they refuse.)

TWO SHEPHERDESSES
(words altered from Dryden).

Shepherd, Shepherd, May invites you,
Tune your pipes this summer's day;
Say, what pastime e'er delights you,
Like our rustic holiday?

Singing, dancing, sporting, toying,
On this smooth and daisied plain;
No dull care our peace destroying
Love and friendship ever reign.

CHORUS.

Come shepherds, lead up a lively measure,
The cares of wedlock are cares of pleasure;
But whether marriage bring joy or sorrow.
Make sure of this day, and hang to-morrow.

(The dance after the song, and exeunt Shepherds and Shepherdesses.)

Oswald, now flying from the Britons, wanders into their camp, and happening to find Emmeline unguarded, carries her off, and in a subsequent scene with Arthur, refuses to restore her. Arthur attempts bribes and threats, but apparently in vain.

ACT III.

Oswald, by magic arts, has spread a panic through the British host, and obtained a victory over Arthur. In an enchanted wood, Philidel, seeking Emmeline, in order that her sight may be restored, is seized by Grimbald, and bound in a chain; but almo ' immediately frees himself by a spell, and succeeds in obtaining the magic vial from Merlin, and in anointing Emmeline's eyes with the contents; (the lyrical numbers with which the restoration of Emmeline's sight is accompanied, though probably set by Purcell, have not been discovered). Her sight is no sooner restored than she is assailed by the magician Osmond who enforces his suit by exhibiting an illustration of the force of love

"in countries caked with ice,
Where the proud god disdaining winter's bounds
O'erleaps the fences of eternal snow,
And with his warmth supplies the distant sun.'
"Osmond strikes the ground with his wand; the scene changes to a prospect of Winter in frozen countries. Cupid descends."

FROST SCENE.

CUPID.

What ho, thou Genius of this clime, what ho!
Liest thou asleep beneath those hills of snow?
Stretch out thy lazy limbs; awake, awake!
And winter from thy furry mantle shake.

(Cold Genius arises.)

COLD GENIUS.

What power art thou, who from below
Hast made me rise unwillingly and slow
From beds of everlasting snow?
Seest thou not how stiff and wondrous old,
Far unfit to bear the bitter cold?
I can scarcely move or draw my breath;
Let me, let me freeze again to death.

CUPID.

Thou doting fool, forbear, forbear;
What? dost thou dream of freezing here?
At Love's appearing, all the sky clearing,
The stormy winds their fury spare;
Winter subduing, and spring renewing,
   My beams create a more glorious year.

COLD GENIUS.

Great Love, I know thee now;
Eldest of the gods art thou;
Heaven and earth by thee were made.
   Human nature
   Is thy creature,
Everywhere thou art obeyed.

CUPID.

No part of my dominion shall be waste;
   To spread my sway and sing my praise
   E'en here I will a people raise
Of kind embracing lovers and embraced.

("Cupid waves his wand, upon which the scene opens and discovers a prospect of ice and snow to the end of the stage. Singers, and dancers, men and women, appear.")

CHORUS.

   See, see, we assemble
   Thy revels to hold,
   Though quivering with cold;
We chatter and tremble.

CUPID.

'Tis I that have warm'd ye.
   In spite of cold weather
   I've brought ye together;
'Tis I that have arm'd ye.

CHORUS.

'Tis Love that has warm'd us;
   In spite of cold weather
   He brought us together;
'Tis Love that has arm'd us.

CUPID and GENIUS.

Sound a parley, ye fair, and surrender,
   Set yourselves and your lovers at ease
He's a grateful offender
   Who pleasure dare seize;
But the whining pretender
   Is sure to displease.

Since the fruit of desire is possessing,
   'Tis unmanly to sigh and complain:
When we kneel for redressing
   We move your disdain;
Love was made for a blessing
   And not for a pain.

ACT IV.

SYLVAN SCENE.

Osmond and Grimbald prepare a further series of enchantments in order to obtain possession of Arthur, who has undertaken to destroy the enchanted wood. Merlin cannot enter the magic grove, but gives his wand to Philidel, bidding him watch over the king in his course through the forest. As he passes over a golden bridge across a river, two sirens rise from the water, and sing; (the first song, "O pass not on, but stay", is one of the lost numbers).

DUET.

Two daughters of this aged stream are we;
And both our sea-green locks have combed
                    for thee.
   Come bathe with us an hour or two,
   What danger from a naked foe?
Come bathe with us, come bathe, and share
What pleasures in the floods appear.
We'll beat the waters till they bound,
And circle round, around, around.

Resisting their allurements, Arthur proceeds on his adventure; the next incident is a dance of nymphs and sylvans with branches in their hands. The number is peculiarly interesting as music, for it is in the form of a passacaglia, with varied treatment of solo voices and chorus.

SOLOS and CHORUS.

   How happy the lover,
   How easy his chain,
   How pleasing his pain!
How sweet to discover
   He sighs not in vain!
For love every creature
Is formed by his nature,
   No joys are above
   The pleasures of love.

   In vain are our graces,
   In vain are your eyes,
   If love you despise;

When age furrows faces
'Tis time to be wise.
Then use the short blessing
That flies in possessing:
No joys are above
The pleasures of love.

Arthur now begins his work of hewing down the grove, but at the first stroke blood spouts from the tree, a shriek is heard, and the form of Emmeline appears, with her arm wounded; she represents herself as imprisoned in the tree by Osmond, and offers herself to his embraces. At this juncture, Philidel appears, touches her with the wand, and reveals Grimbald who has assumed her form. The evil spirit is now bound in his turn, and the destruction of the wood is accomplished with a few strokes.

ACT V.

The struggle between the opposing forces reaches its height in a personal encounter between Arthur and Oswald, each aided by his own magician. The former is of course victorious, and Emmeline is restored to Arthur. As a conclusion of the play, Merlin shews to the assembled characters a prophetic

VISION OF BRITAIN.

"Merlin waves his wand, the scene changes and discovers the British Ocean in a storm. Aeolus in a cloud above; four winds hanging, &c."

AEOLUS.

Ye blustering brethren of the skies,
  Whose breath has ruffled all the watery plain,
Retire, and let Britannia rise,
  In triumph o'er the main.
Serene and calm and void of fear,
The queen of islands must appear.

(The remainder of this song was not set.)

"Aeolus ascends and the four winds fly off; the scene opens and discovers a calm sea to the end of the house. An island arises to a soft tune, Britannia seated in the island with fishermen at her feet, etc.; the tune changes, the fishermen come ashore and dance awhile, after which Pan and a Nereid come on the stage and sing."

DUET & CHORUS.

Round thy coasts, fair nymph of Britain,
  For thy guard our waters flow;
Proteus all his herd admitting
  On thy greens to graze below.
Foreign lands thy fishes tasting
Learn from thee luxurious fasting.

TRIO.

For folded flocks on fruitful plains,
  The shepherd's and the farmer's gains,
  Fair Britain all the world outvies;
And Pan as in Arcadia reigns,
  Where pleasure mixed with profit lies.

Though Jason's fleece was famed of old,
The British wool is growing gold;
  No mines can more of wealth supply;
It keeps the peasant from the cold,
And takes for kings the Tyrian dye.

"Enter Comus with three peasants, who sing the following song in parts."

COMUS.

Your hay it is mow'd and your corn is reaped;
Your barns will be full, and your hovels heaped;
  Come, my boys, come:
And merrily roar out harvest home.

Chorus, Harvest home, &c.

We'll toss off our ale till we cannot stand,
And heigh for the honour of old England.

Chorus, Old England &c.

Enter Venus, who sings.

VENUS.

Fairest Isle, all isles excelling,
  Seat of pleasures and of loves,
Venus here will choose her dwelling,
  And forsake her Cyprian groves.
Cupid, from his favourite nation
  Care and envy will remove;
Jealousy, that poisons passion,
  And despair that dies for love.

Gentle murmurs, sweet complaining,
  Sighs that blow the fire of love;
Soft repulses, kind disdaining,
  Shall be all the pains you prove.
Every swain shall pay his duty,
  Grateful every nymph shall prove;
And as these excel in beauty,
  Those shall be renowned for love.

DIALOGUE, nymph and shepherd.

SHE.

You say 'tis love creates the pain
Of which so sadly you complain;
And yet would fain engage my heart
In that uneasy cruel part.

But how, alas, think you that I
Can bear the wound of which you die?

HE.

'Tis not my passion makes my care,
But your indifference gives despair;
The lusty sun begets no spring,
Till gentle showers assistance bring;
So love, that scorches and destroys,
Till kindness aid, can cause no joys.

SHE.

Love has a thousand ways to please,
But more to rob us of our ease;
For wakeful nights and careful days
Some hours of pleasure he repays;
But absence soon, or jealous fears,
O'erflow the joys with floods of tears.

HE.

By vain and senseless forms betrayed,
Harmless love's the offender made;
While we no other pains endure
Than those that we ourselves procure;]
But one soft moment makes amends
For all the torment that attends.

BOTH.

Let us love, and to happiness haste;
Age and wisdom come too fast;
Youth for loving was designed,

HE.

I'll be constant, you be kind

SHE.

You be constant, I'll be kind.

BOTH.

Heaven can give no greater blessing
Than faithful love and kind possessing.

"After the dialogue, a warlike concert; the scene opens, above, and discovers the order of the Garter. Enter Honour, attended by Heroes."

HONOUR.

Saint George, the patron of our isle,
 A soldier and a saint,
On that auspicious order smile
 Which love and arms will plant.

CHORUS.

Our natives not alone appear
 To court this martial prize;
But foreign kings, adopted here,
 Their crowns at home despise.

Our sovereign high, in awful state,
 His honours shall bestow;
And see his sceptred subjects wait
 On his commends below.

"A full chorus of the whole song, after which the grand dance."

THE END.

KING ARTHUR.

OVERTURE.

HENRY PURCELL.

ACT I.
SACRIFICE SCENE.

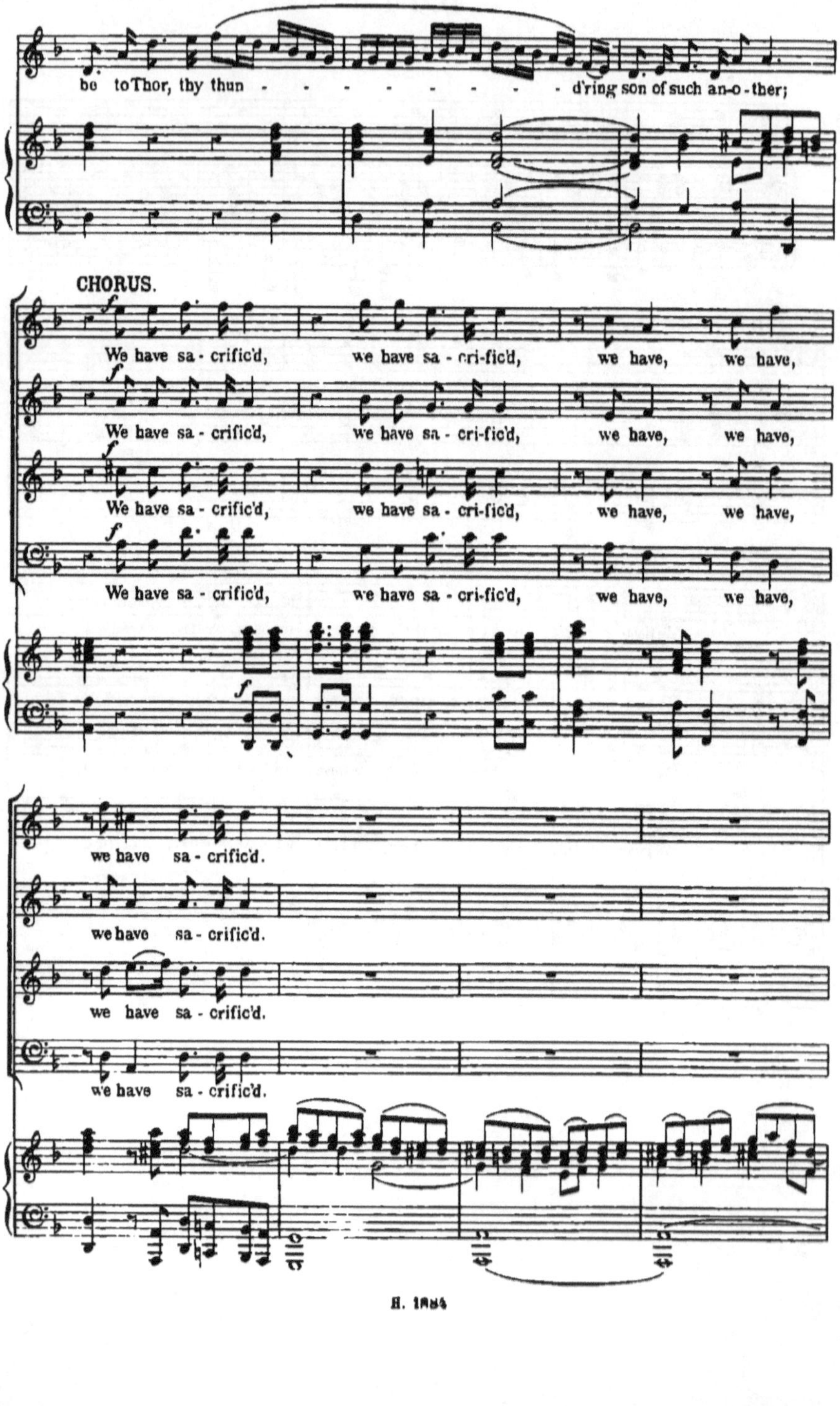
be to Thor, thy thun - - - - - - - - - - d'ring son of such an-o-ther;
CHORUS.
We have sa-crific'd, we have sa-cri-fic'd, we have, we have,
We have sa-crific'd, we have sa-cri-fic'd, we have, we have,
We have sa-crific'd, we have sa-cri-fic'd, we have, we have,
We have sa-crific'd, we have sa-cri-fic'd, we have, we have,
we have sa-crific'd.
we have sa-crific'd.
we have sa-crific'd.
we have sa-crific'd.

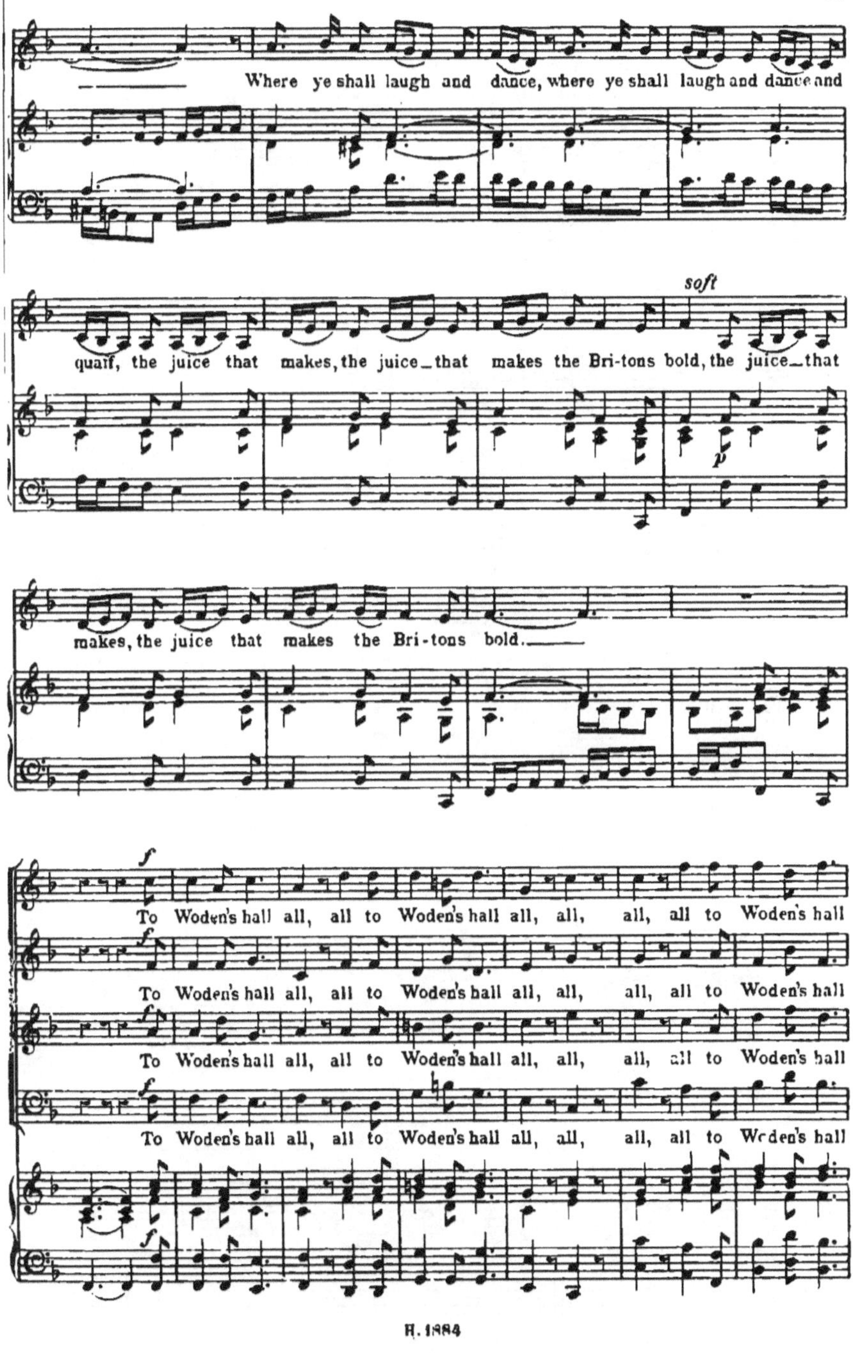
Where ye shall laugh and dance, where ye shall laugh and dance and
quaff, the juice that makes, the juice_that makes the Bri-tons bold, the juice_that
soft
p
makes, the juice that makes the Bri-tons bold.
f
To Woden's hall all, all to Woden's hall all, all, all, all to Woden's hall
To Woden's hall all, all to Woden's hall all, all, all, all to Woden's hall
To Woden's hall all, all to Woden's hall all, all, all, all to Woden's hall
To Woden's hall all, all to Woden's hall all, all, all, all to Woden's hall

BATTLE SCENE.

Nº 4. Tenor Solo and Chorus.

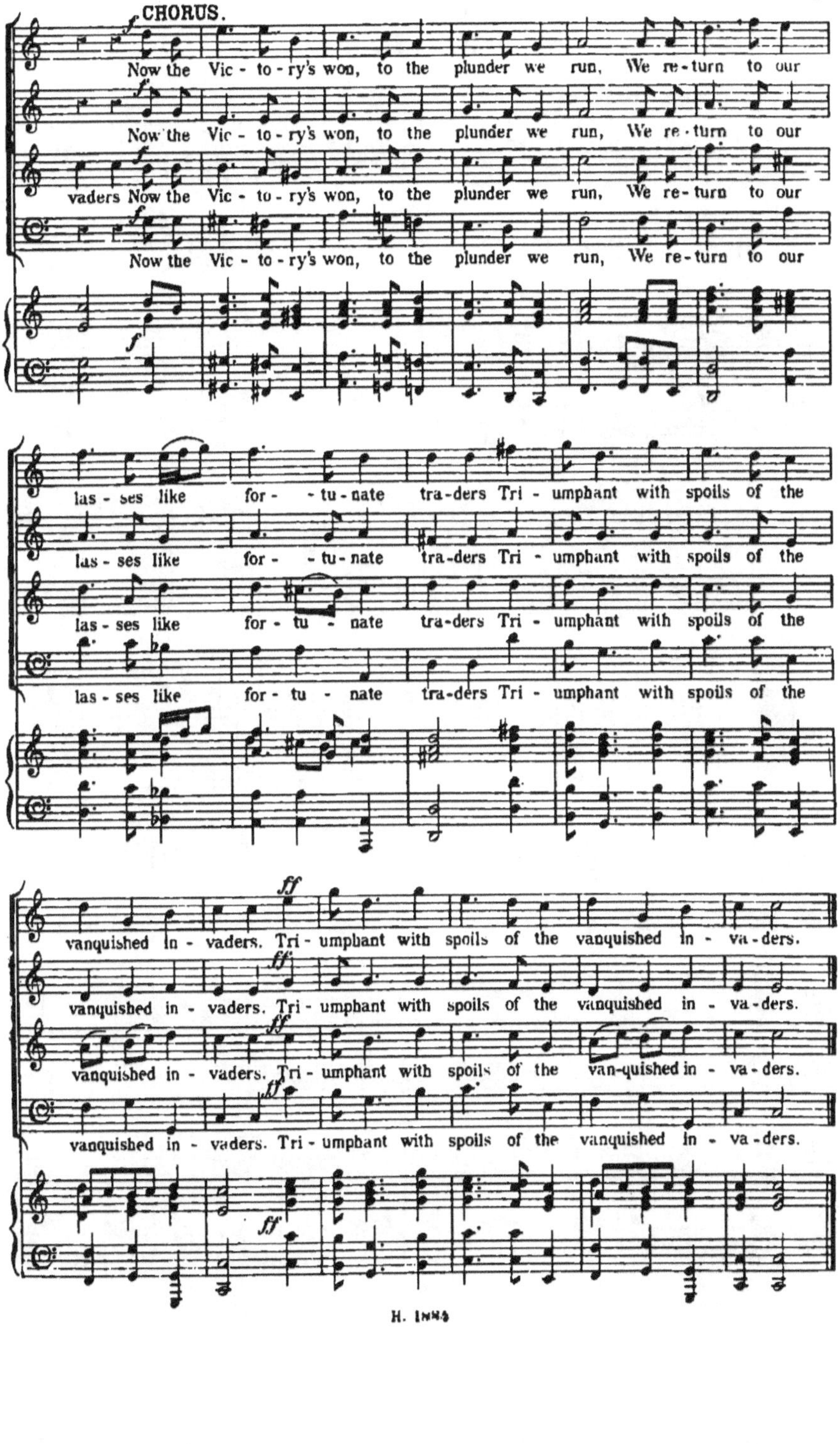
CHORUS.
f
Now the Vic-to-ry's won, to the plunder we run, We re-turn to our
Now the Vic-to-ry's won, to the plunder we run, We re-turn to our
vaders Now the Vic-to-ry's won, to the plunder we run, We re-turn to our
Now the Vic-to-ry's won, to the plunder we run, We re-turn to our
las-ses like for- -tu-nate tra-ders Tri-umphant with spoils of the
las-ses like for- -tu-nate tra-ders Tri-umphant with spoils of the
las-ses like for-tu-nate tra-ders Tri-umphant with spoils of the
las-ses like for-tu-nate tra-ders Tri-umphant with spoils of the
ff
vanquished in-vaders. Tri-umphant with spoils of the vanquished in-va-ders.
vanquished in-vaders. Tri-umphant with spoils of the vanquished in-va-ders.
vanquished in-vaders. Tri-umphant with spoils of the van-quished in-va-ders.
vanquished in-vaders. Tri-umphant with spoils of the vanquished in-va-ders.

No 7. Solo and Chorus.

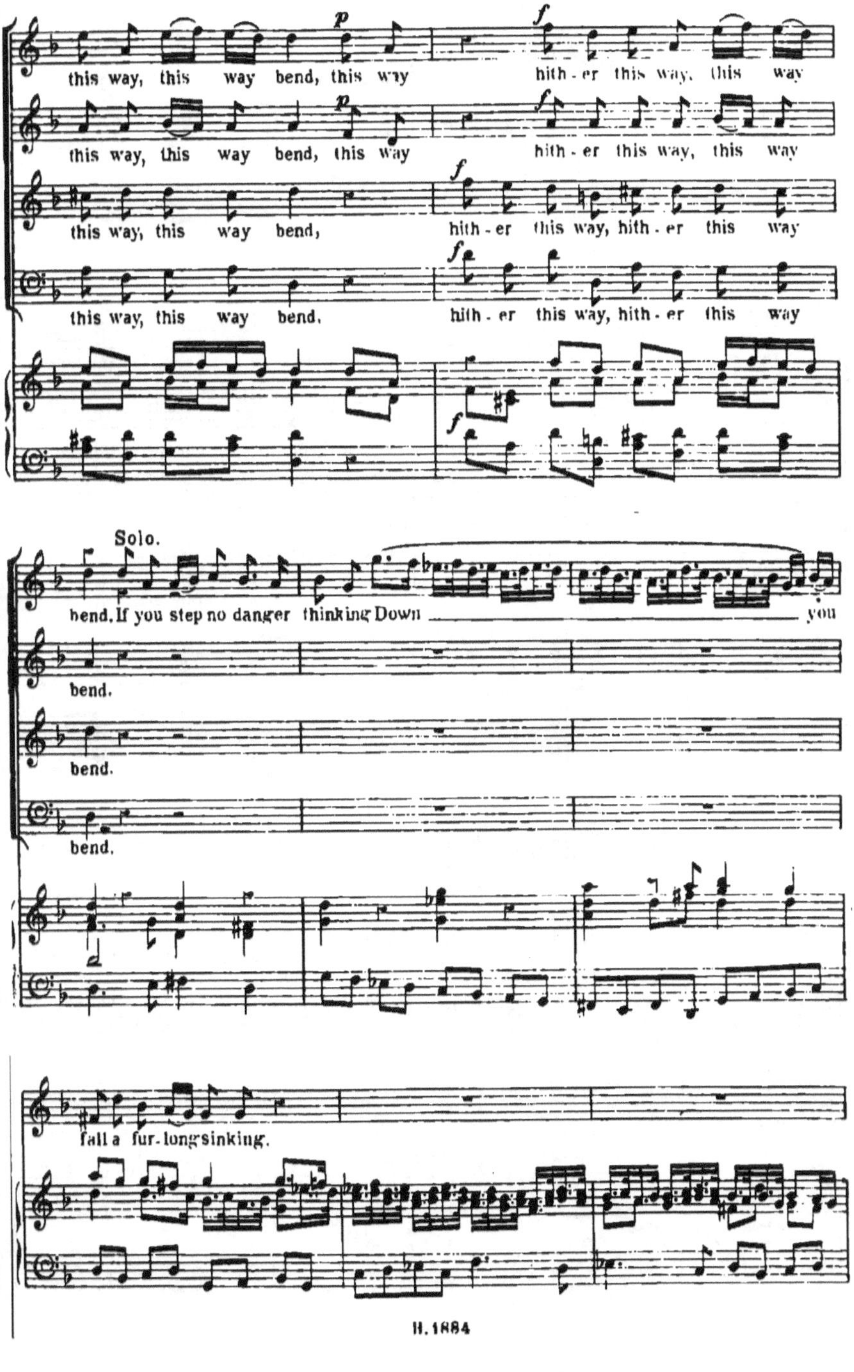
this way, this way bend, this way hith-er this way, this way
this way, this way bend, this way hith-er this way, this way
this way, this way bend, hith-er this way, hith-er this way
this way, this way bend, hith-er this way, hith-er this way
Solo.
bend, If you step no danger thinking Down you
bend.
bend.
bend.
fall a fur-long sinking.

No 9. Chorus.

Nº 10. Quintet and Chorus.
Philidel's Spirits.

No. 12. Duet. (2 SOPRANOS.)

No 13. Chorus.

ACT III.
FROST SCENE.
No. 15. Recit. and Solos. (Soprano and Bass.)

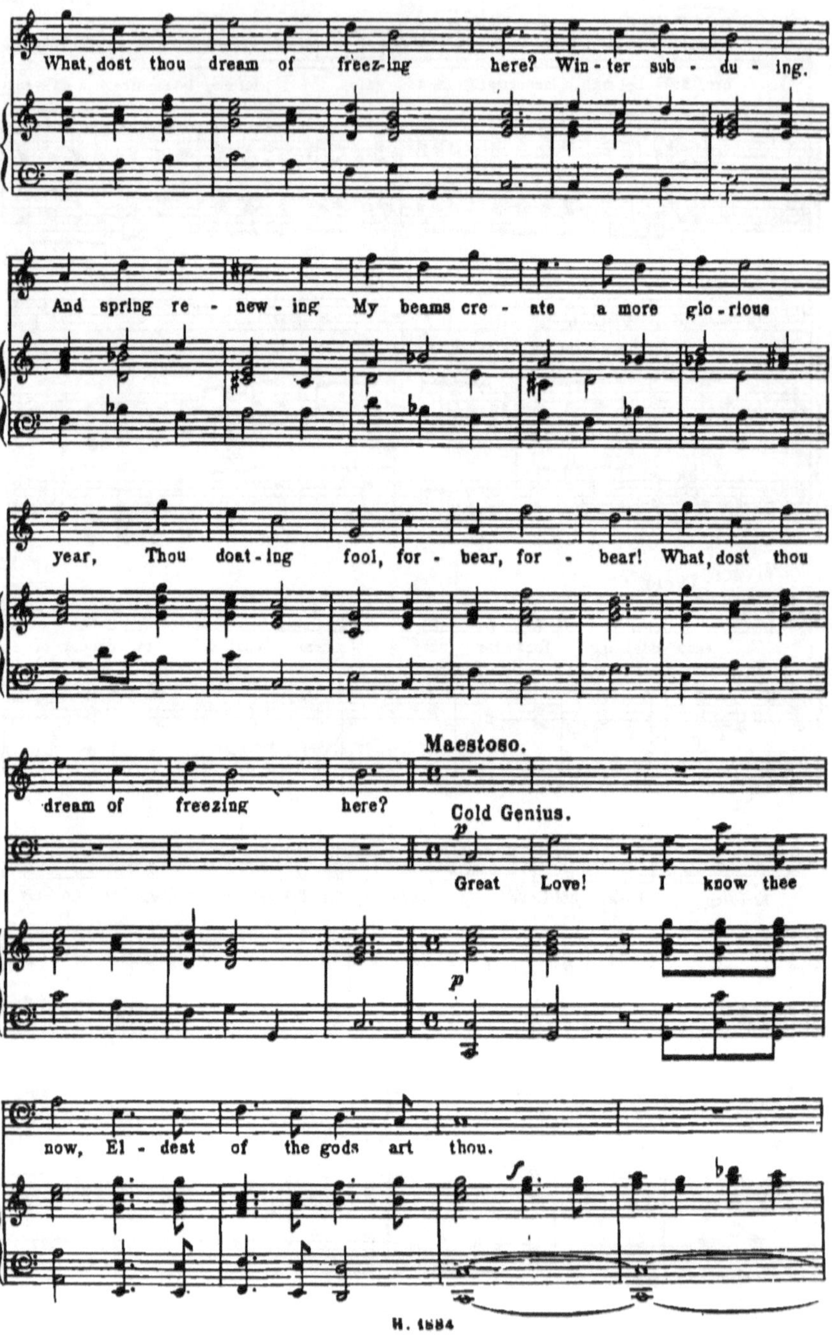
What, dost thou dream of freez-ing here? Win-ter sub-du-ing.
And spring re-new-ing My beams cre-ate a more glo-rious
year, Thou doat-ing fool, for-bear, for-bear! What, dost thou
dream of freezing here?
Maestoso.
Cold Genius.
p
Great Love! I know thee
p
now, El-dest of the gods art thou.

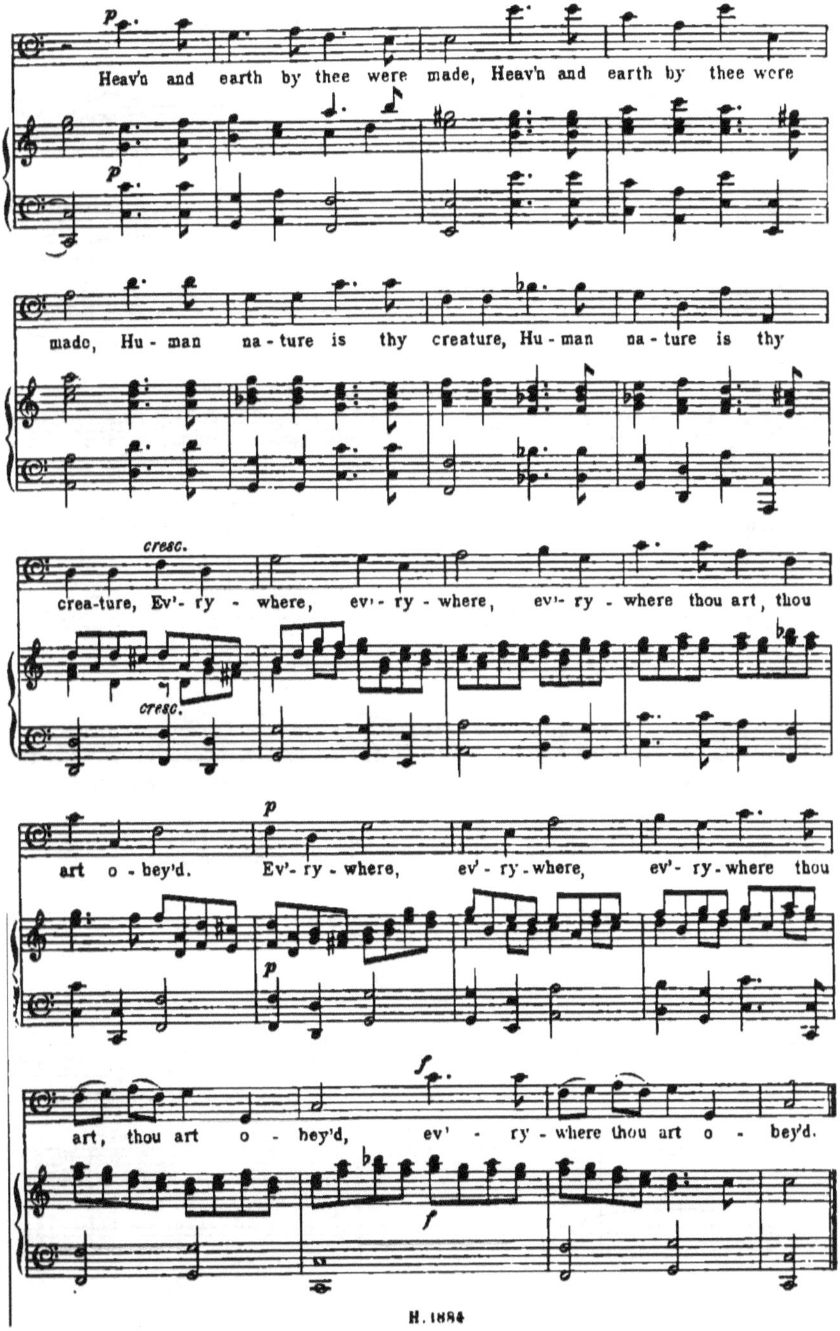
p
Heav'n and earth by thee were made, Heav'n and earth by thee were
made, Hu - man na - ture is thy creature, Hu - man na - ture is thy
cresc.
crea-ture, Ev'- ry - where, ev'- ry - where, ev'- ry - where thou art, thou
art o - bey'd. Ev'- ry - where, ev'- ry - where, ev'- ry - where thou
art, thou art o - bey'd, ev' - ry - where thou art o - bey'd.

Prelude.
Maestoso.

No. 17. Duet.

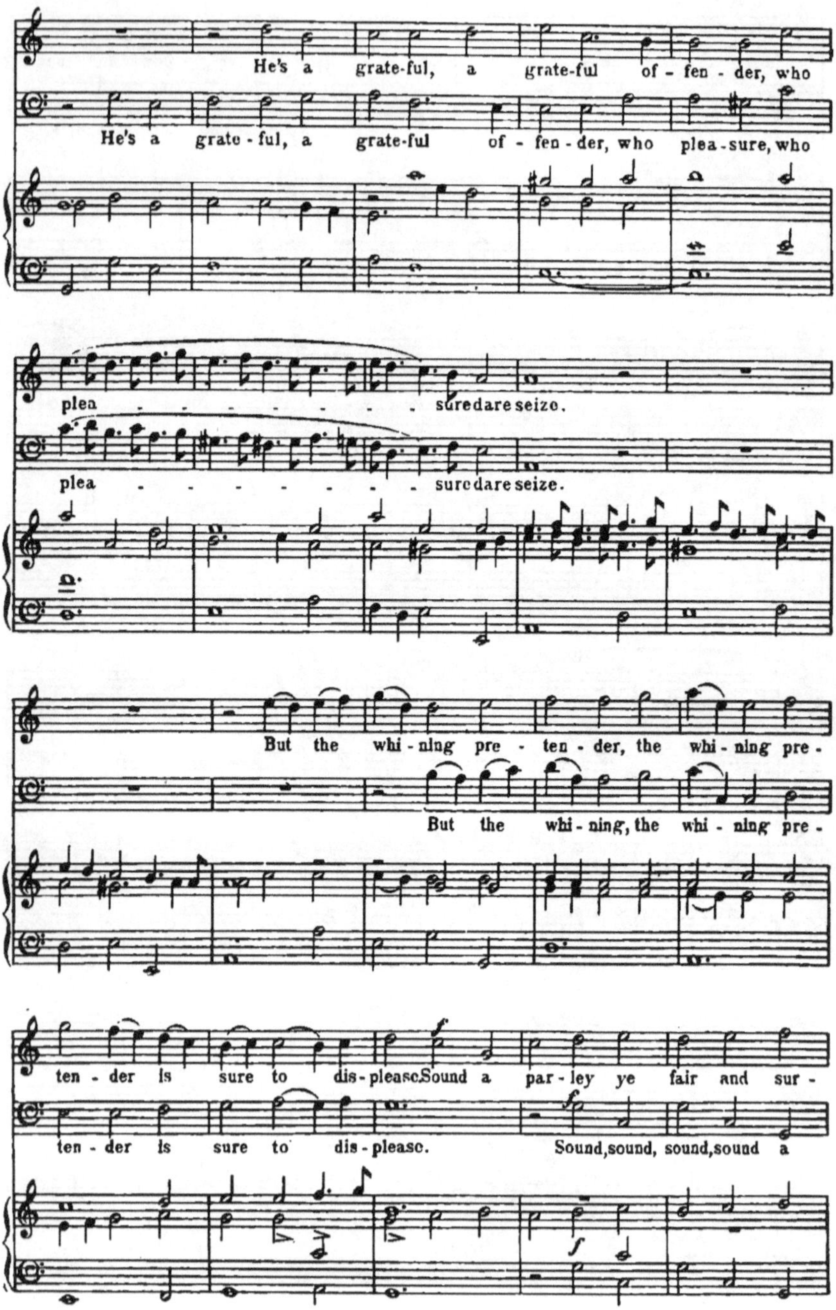
He's a grate-ful, a grate-ful of - fen - der, who
He's a grate - ful, a grate-ful of - fen - der, who plea - sure, who
plea - - - - - - - - - suredare seize.
plea - - - - - - - - - suredare seize.
But the whi - ning pre - ten - der, the whi - ning pre -
But the whi - ning, the whi - ning pre -
ten - der is sure to dis - pleaseSound a par - ley ye fair and sur -
ten - der is sure to dis - please. Sound, sound, sound, sound a

ren - - der, Sound, sound, sound, sound a par - ley ye fair, Sound
par - ley ye fair and sur - ren - - der, Sound a par - ley ye
a par - ley ye fair and sur - ren - der.
fair, sound a par - - - - ley ye fair and sur - ren - der.
mf
Since the fruit of de - sire is pos-ses-sing 'tis un-
mf
Since the fruit of de - sire is pos - ses - sing 'tis un-
mf
man - ly to sigh, 'tis un - man - ly to sigh and com - plain.
man - ly to sigh, 'tis un - man - ly to sigh and com - plain.

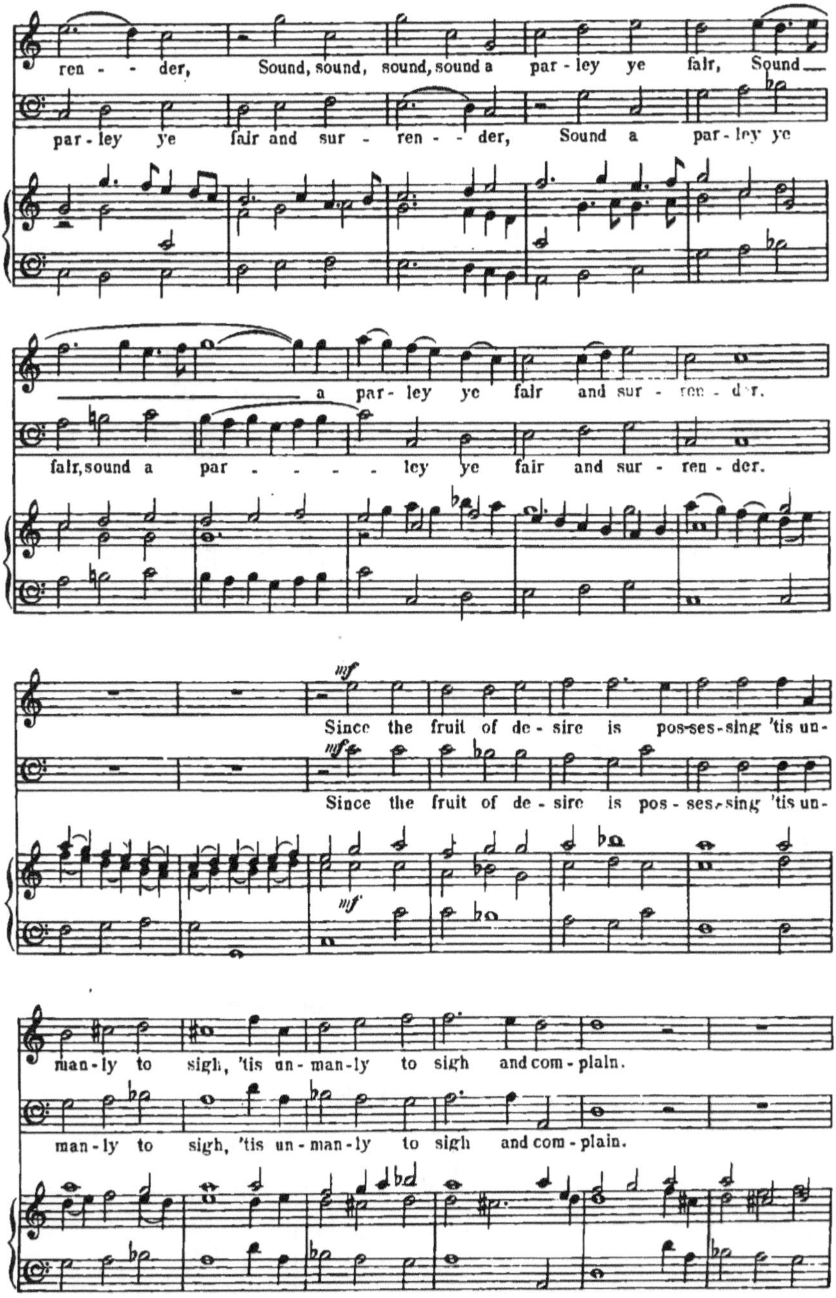

ACT IV.
N⁰ 19. Overture.

No. 21. Passacaglia. (Solos and Chorus.)

ACT V.
THE VISION OF BRITAIN.
Nº 22. Trumpet Tune.

Nº 23. Air.

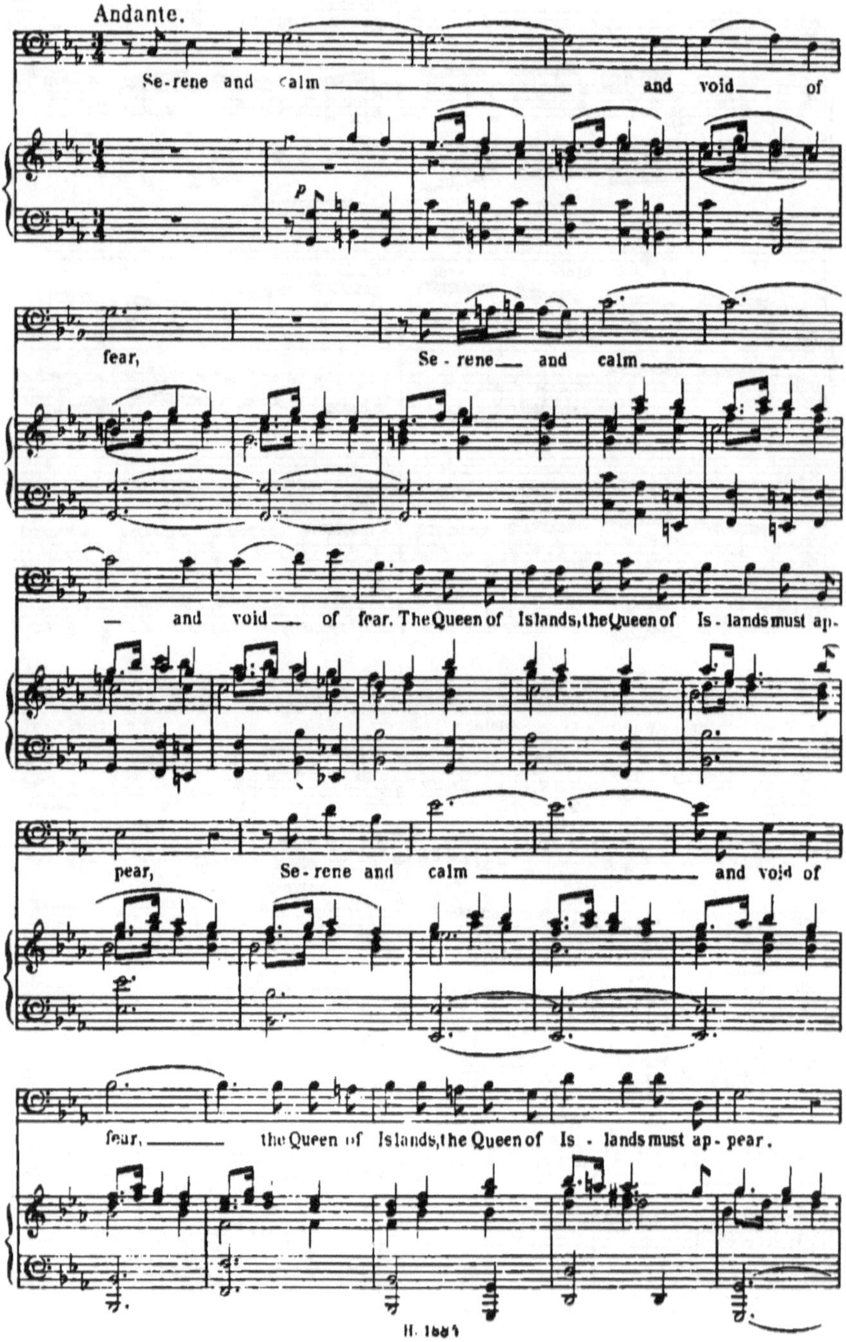
Andante.
Se-rene and calm and void of
fear,
Se-rene and calm
and void of fear. The Queen of Islands, the Queen of Is-lands must ap-
pear,
Se-rene and calm and void of
fear, the Queen of Islands, the Queen of Is-lands must ap-pear.
p

No 25. Symphony.

No. 26. Duet and Chorus.

№ 27. Trio.

No. 28. Song.

No. 29. Song.

N<u>o</u> 30. Dialogue.

SCENE. The Order of the Garter.

Nº 31. Trumpet Tune.

Allegro.

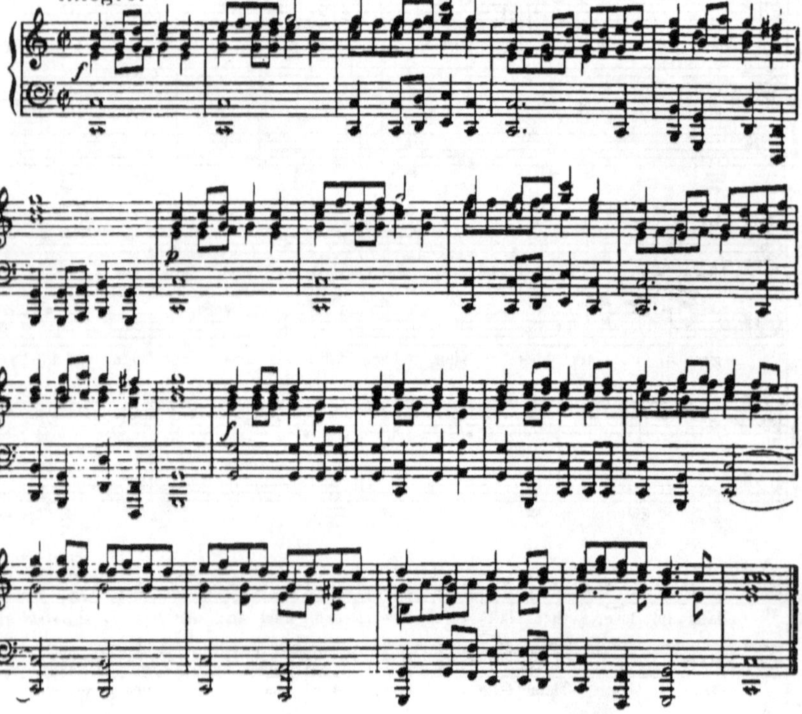

Nº 32. Song.

Allegretto.

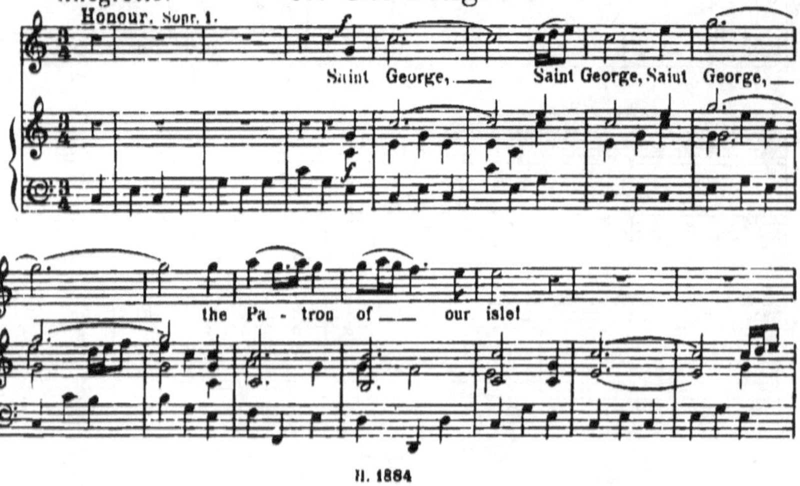
Honour. Sopr. 1.
Saint George, — Saint George, Saint George, —
the Pa - tron of — our isle!

No. 34. The Grand Dance. (Chaconne.)

VOCAL ALBUMS

* **BOOSEY'S COMMUNITY SONG BOOK.** English, Scotch, Welsh, Irish Songs, Rounds, etc.
* **CLUB SONG BOOK, The.** Separate Editions for Boys and Girls.
ELIZABETHAN LOVE SONGS. Frederick Keel. For high or low voice. Two sets of 60 Songs, arranged with piano accompaniment adapted from the lute tablature.
FIFTY MODERN ENGLISH SONGS. Songs by 20th Century Composers.
GOLDEN TREASURY OF SONG. 83 Songs by Classical Composers in 2 Vols.
HANDEL'S OPERA SONGS. 52 Arias, edited by W. T. Best. Italian-English (R.E.)
HANDEL'S ORATORIO SONGS. 72 Arias edited by W. T. Best (R.E.).
HANDEL'S SONGS. Selected and edited by Walter Ford and R. Erlebach. 7 vols.
    Vol. 1 : Light Soprano.   Vol. 2 : Dramatic Soprano.   Vol. 3 : Mezzo-Soprano.
    Vol. 4 : Contralto.   Vol. 5 : Tenor.   Vol. 6 : Baritone.   Vol. 7 : Bass.
IRELAND'S SONGS. A collection of 61 Standard and Popular Songs.
IRISH COUNTRY SONGS. Herbert Hughes. 4 Vols.
IRISH FOLK SONGS. 25 Songs, edited by Charles Wood.
IRISH MELODIES OF THOMAS MOORE, The. Op..60. C. Villiers Stanford.
MANX NATIONAL SONGS. 51 Songs, edited by W. H. Gill (R.E.)
MOZART'S SONGS AND ARIAS. With German, Italian and English Words. Edited by J. Pittman and M. B. Foster (R.E.)
* **NATIONAL SONG BOOK.** Vol 2. 30 Old English Songs, edited by Harold Boulton and Arthur Somervell.
* **NEW NATIONAL SONG BOOK.** Vol. 1. 313 Folk Songs, Carols and Rounds, edited by C. Villiers Stanford, with revised piano accompaniments by the late Dr. J. Shaw.
OLD ENGLISH MELODIES. H. Lane Wilson. 21 Songs by Dr. Arne, Thomas Brown, Carey Dibdin, Hook, Leveridge, Smart, Young, etc.
OLD IRISH MELODIES. Herbert Hughes. 12 Songs.
PICK OF THE BUNCH. Eight Albums of Famous Songs.
    Vol. 1 : 7 Songs for Soprano.   Vol. 2 : 8 Songs for Tenor.
    Vol. 3 : 8 Songs for Mezzo-Soprano.   Vol. 4 : 8 Songs for Baritone.
    Vol 5 : 8 Songs for Contralto.   Vol. 6 : 6 Soldiers' Songs.
    Vol. 7 : 6 Sailors' Songs.   Vol. 8 : Seven Popular Humorous Songs for Baritone.
RUBINSTEIN'S SONGS. Fifty-nine Songs with German and English Words. (R.E.)
SAILORS' SONGS OR CHANTIES. Ferris Tozer. 50 Songs.
SELECT FRENCH SONGS FROM THE 12TH TO THE 18TH CENTURY. Arnold Dolmetsch.
SEVEN SEAS SHANTY BOOK, The. Taylor S. Harris. 42 Sea Shanties collected and recollected by John Sampson.
SONGS FROM MANY LANDS (Liedere van baie nasies). Helen V. S. Roberts. 24 Songs. English-Afrikaans.
SONGS FROM THE OPERAS. 50 Arias for Tenor and Baritone edited by J. Pittman (R.E.)
SONGS OF BRITAIN. Selected and edited by Frank Kidson and Martin Shaw. 100 English, Welsh, Scottish, and Irish Songs.
SONGS OF ENGLAND. 279 Songs edited by J. L. Hatton and E. Faning (R.E.) 3 Vols.
SONGS OF THE HEBRIDES. 156 Songs in 3 Vols. edited by Marjory and Patuffa Kennedy-Fraser. Also 3 Vols. of "Twelve Selected Songs of the Hebrides". For High or Low Voice
SONGS OF IRELAND. 87 Songs edited by J. L. Hatton and J. L. Molloy (R.E.)
SONGS OF ITALY. 54 Popular Italian Songs with Italian and English Words (R.E.)
SONGS OF OLD IRELAND. C. Villiers Stanford. 50 Old Irish Melodies.
SONGS OF SCANDINAVIA and Northern Europe. Edited by J. A. Kappey (R.E.) 84 Songs from Holland, Scandinavia, Finland, Russia and Poland.
SONGS OF SCOTLAND. 240 Songs edited by C. Brown, J. Pittman, M. B. Foster (R.E.). 2 Vols.
SONGS OF WALES. 70 Songs edited by Brinley Richards, English-Welsh (R.E.)
WELSH MELODIES. St. David's Edition. 32 Songs edited by J. Lloyd Williams and Arthur Somervell. With traditional and original Welsh words and English Lyrics by A. P. Graves. 2 Vols. (Vol. 1 for High or Low Voice. Vol. 2 for Low or Medium Voice only.)

* *Words and Melody Editions also available*
Abbreviation : (R.E.) Royal Edition.
For Prices see Current Catalogue.

BOOSEY & HAWKES
LIMITED
295 Regent Street, London, W.1
New York · Los Angeles · Sydney · Capetown · Toronto · Paris

www.ingramcontent.com/pod-product-compliance
Lightning Source LLC
Chambersburg PA
CBHW020101170426
43199CB00009B/365